I Can See

Julie Murray

Abdo
SENSES
Kids

abdopublishing.com

Published by Abdo Kids, a division of ABDO, PO Box 398166, Minneapolis, Minnesota 55439.
Copyright © 2016 by Abdo Consulting Group, Inc. International copyrights reserved in all countries.
No part of this book may be reproduced in any form without written permission from the publisher.

Printed in the United States of America, North Mankato, Minnesota.

052015

092015

 THIS BOOK CONTAINS
RECYCLED MATERIALS

Photo Credits: iStock, Shutterstock

Production Contributors: Teddy Borth, Jennie Forsberg, Grace Hansen

Design Contributors: Candice Keimig, Dorothy Toth

Library of Congress Control Number: 2014958411
Cataloging-in-Publication Data
Murray, Julie.
 I can see / Julie Murray.
  p. cm. -- (Senses)
ISBN 978-1-62970-926-0
Includes index.
1. Eye--Juvenile literature. I. Title.
612.8'4--dc23
                    2014958411

Table of Contents

I Can See

There are five senses.

Sight is one of the senses.

We see with our eyes.

We see things all around us!

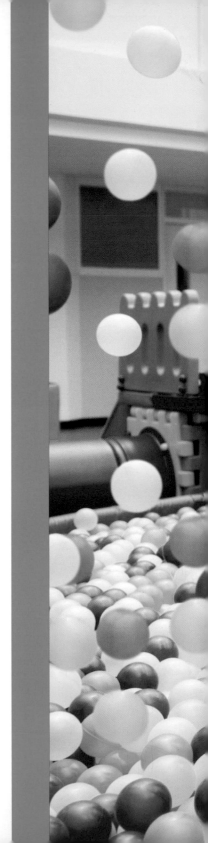

We see during the day.

Jack wears his **sunglasses**.

We see at night.

Nora uses a **telescope**.

We see colors.

Leah sees the flowers.

We see books.

Amy reads with her dad.

We see our friends.

Gus plays football.

We see our family.

Jay plays with his sister.

What did you see today?

21

The Five Senses

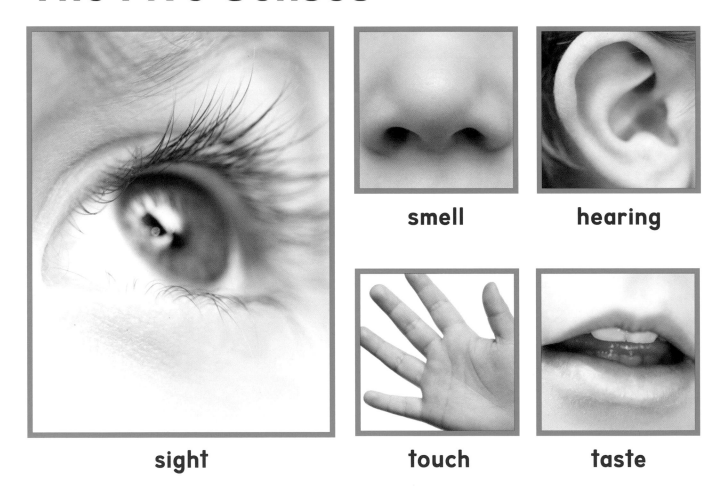

sight

smell

hearing

touch

taste

Glossary

sunglasses
tinted glass worn to protect
the eyes from the sun.

telescope
a tool used to make things that
are very far away seem closer.

Index

abdokids.com

Use this code to log on to abdokids.com and access crafts, games, videos, and more!

Abdo Kids Code:
SIK9260

24